SIMON BOND

A Hundred and One Uses of a Dead Cat

A Hundred and One More Uses of a Dead Cat

Uses of a Dead Cat in History

CHANCELLOR
PRESS

A Hundred and One Uses of a Dead Cat first published in 1981
by Eyre Methuen Limited
A Hundred and One More Uses of a Dead Cat first published in 1982
by Methuen London Limited
Uses of a Dead Cat in History first published in 1992
by Mandarin Paperbacks

This edition first published in 1993 by Chancellor Press
an imprint of Reed Consumer Books Limited
Michelin House, 81 Fulham Road, London SW3 6RB
and Auckland, Melbourne, Singapore and Toronto

ISBN 1 85152 428 2

A CIP catalogue record for this book is available from the British Library

Printed and bound in Slovenia
by Mladinska knjiga

A Hundred and One Uses of a

DEAD·CAT

SIMON BOND

Mandarin
81 Fulham Road
London S.W.3

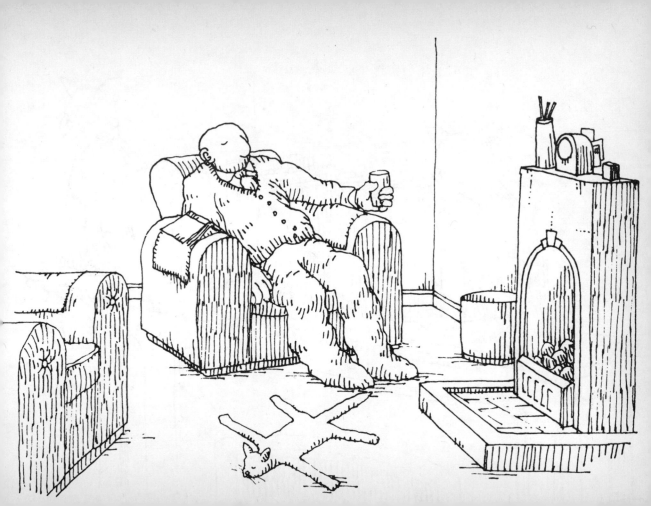

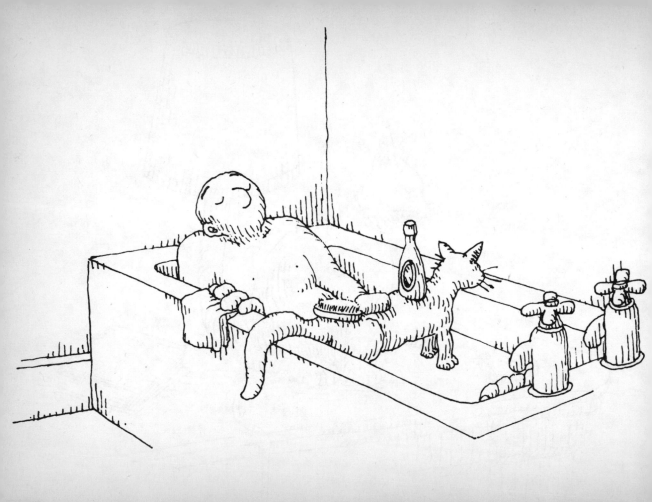

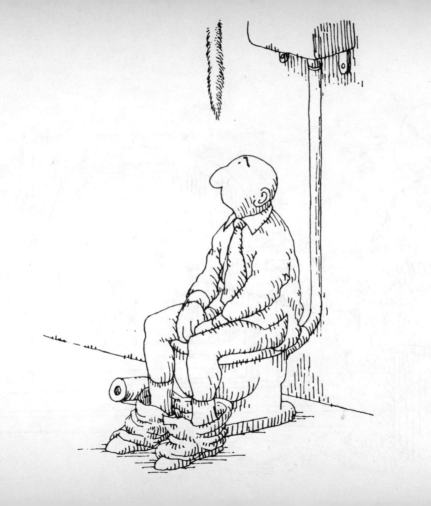

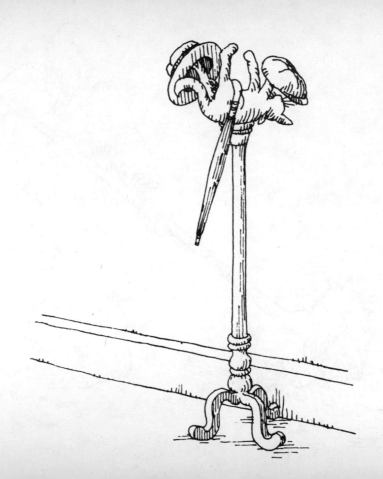

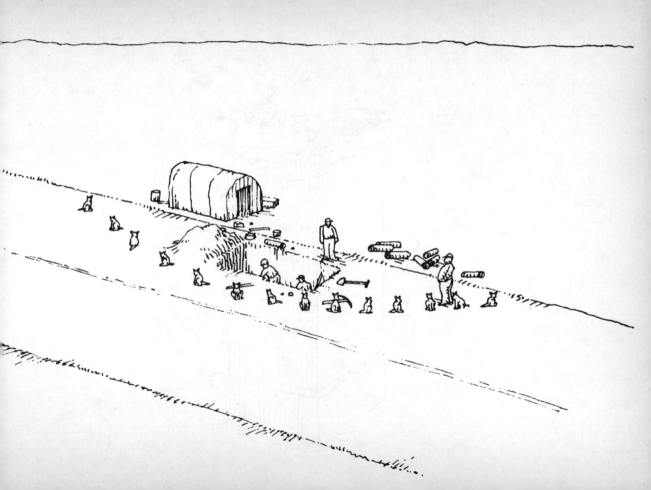

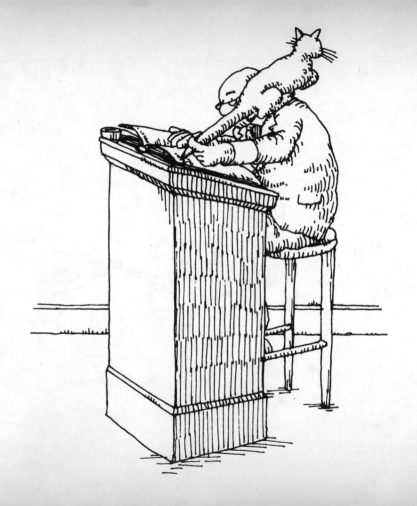

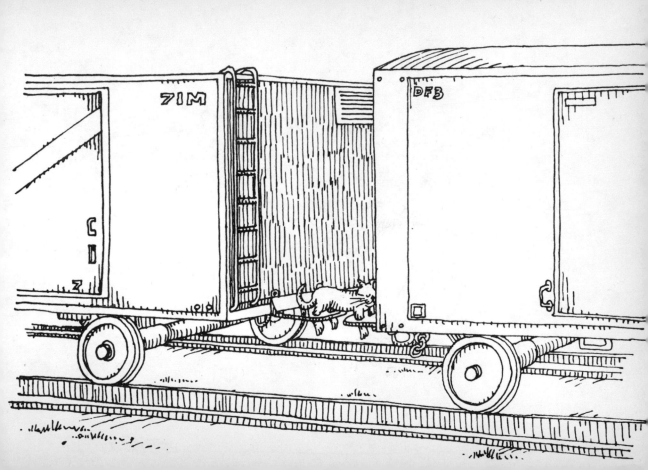

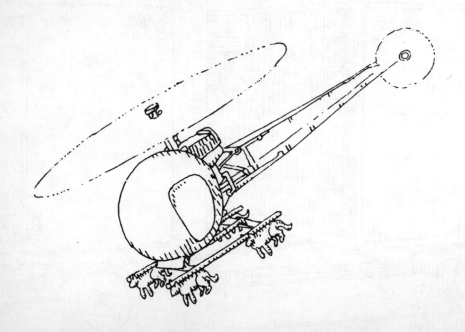

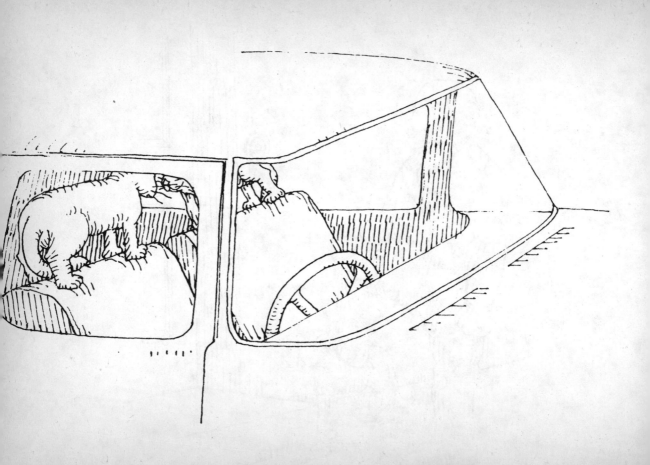

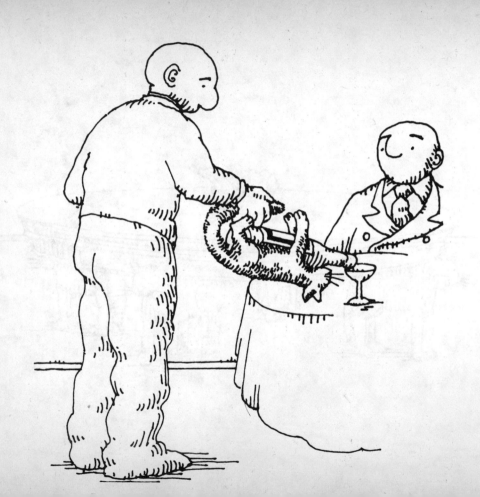

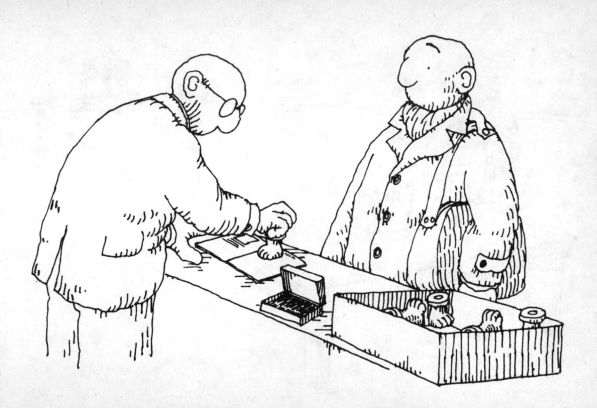

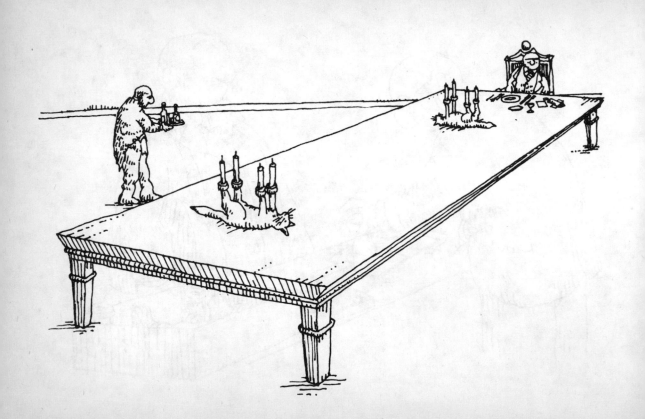

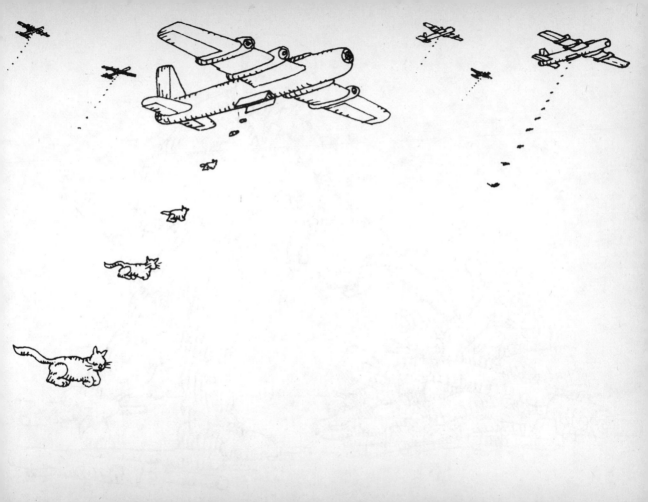

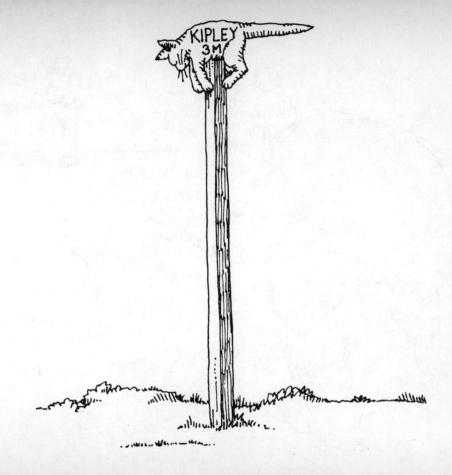

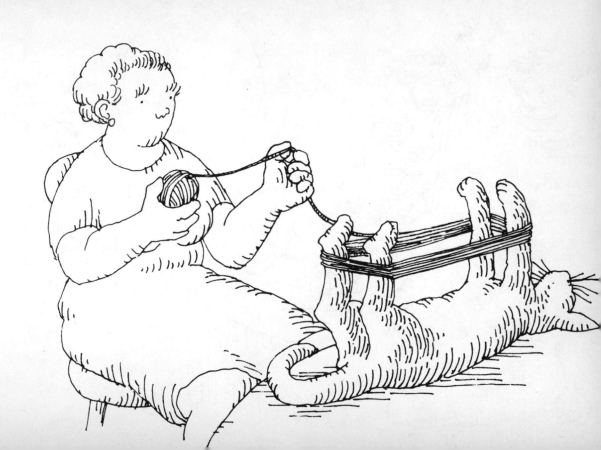

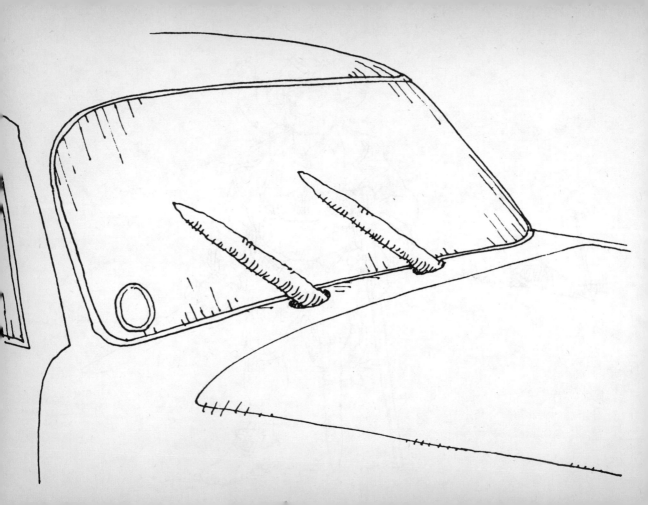

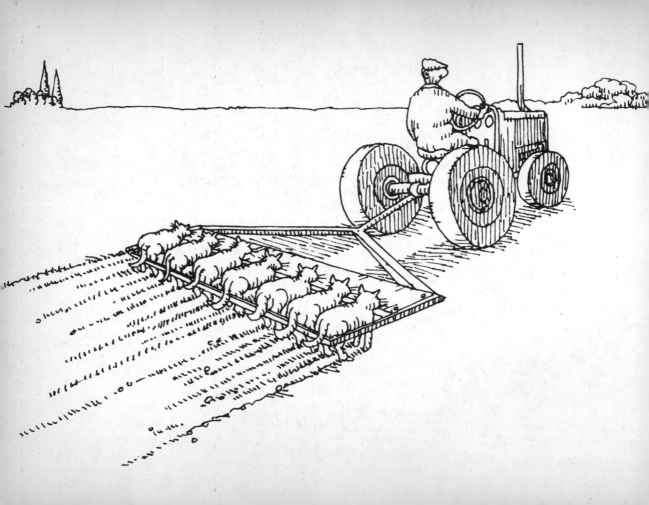

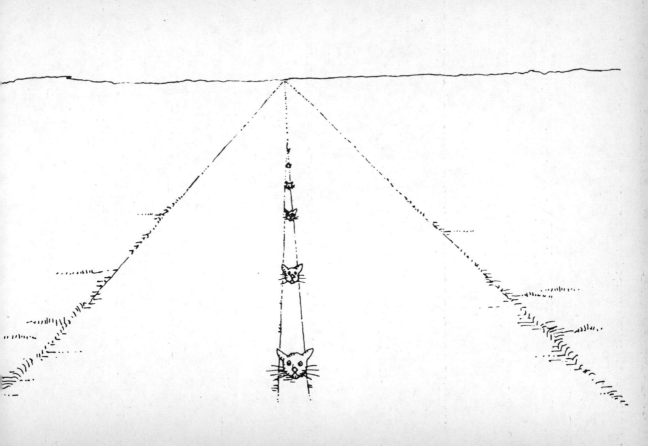

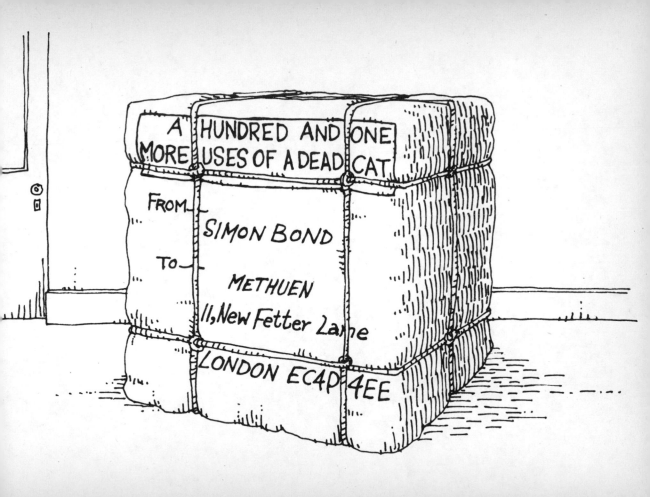

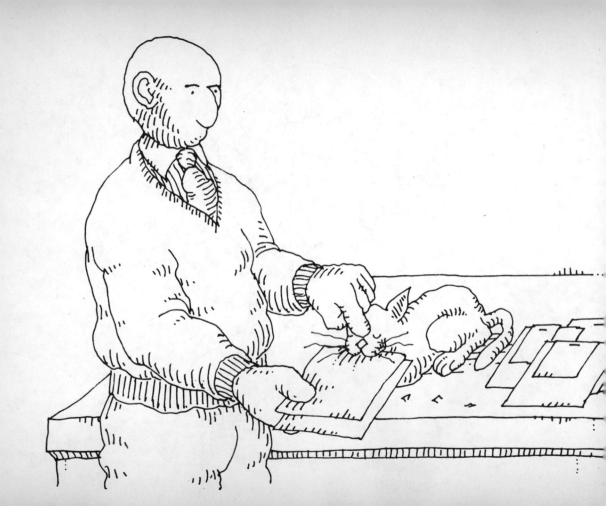

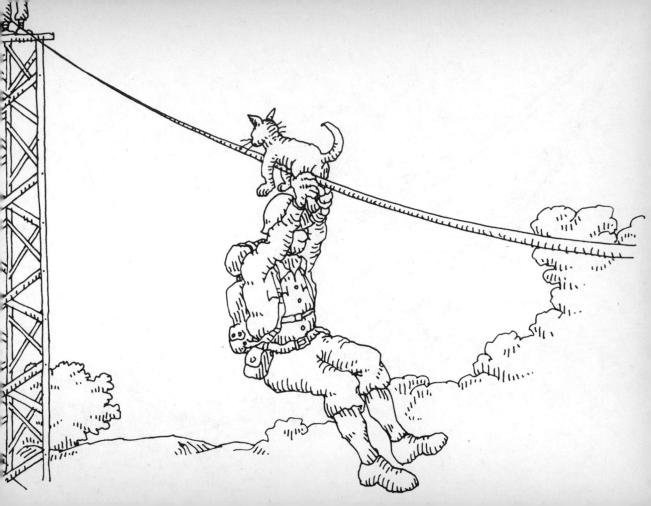

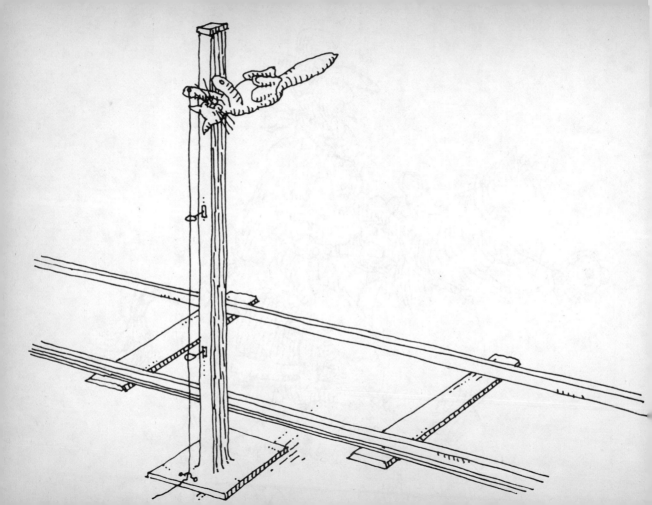

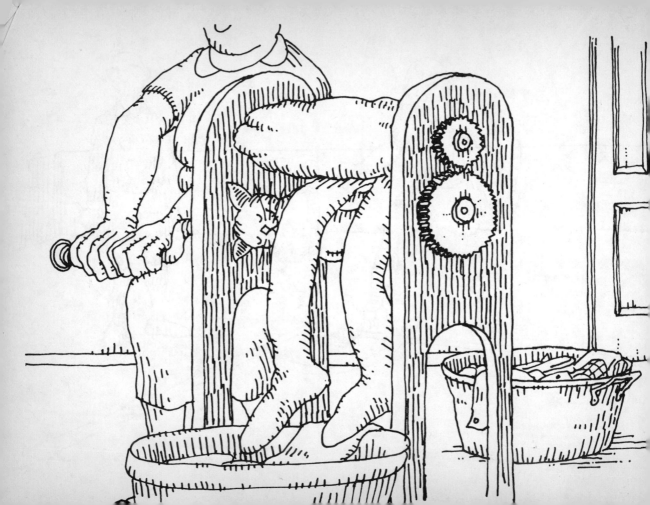

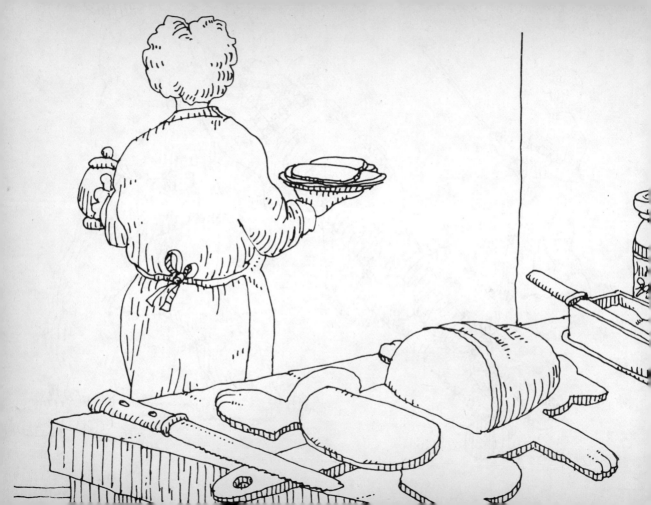

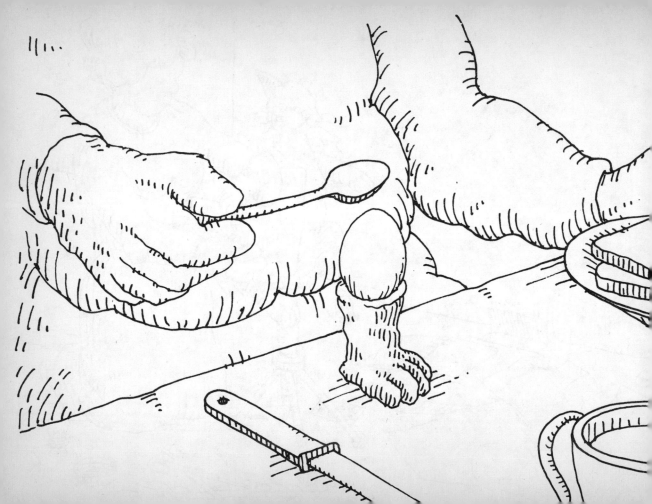

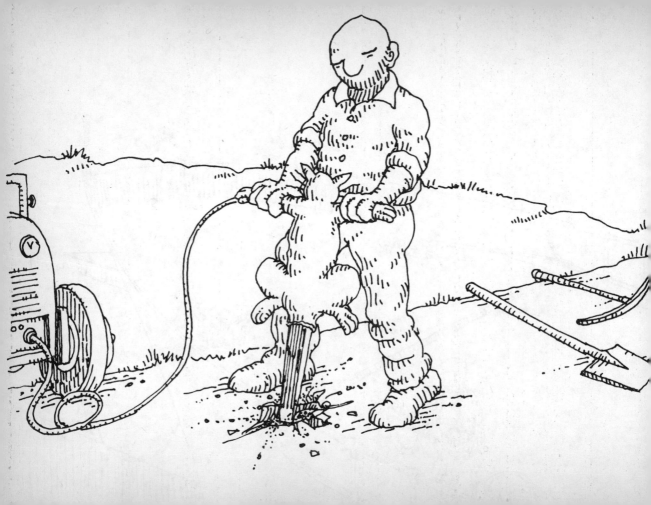

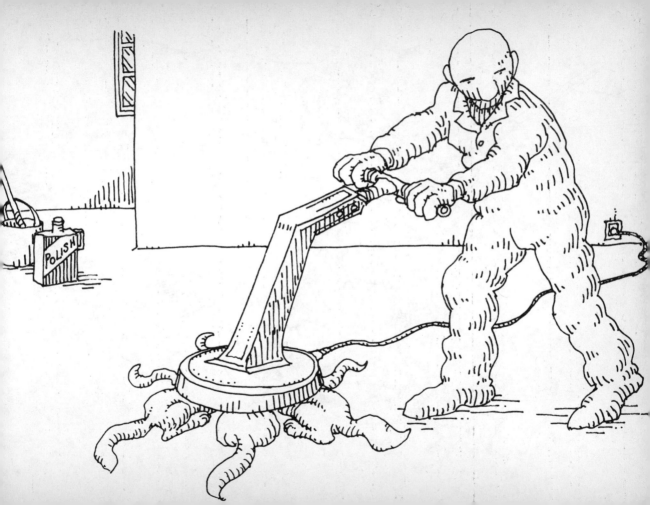

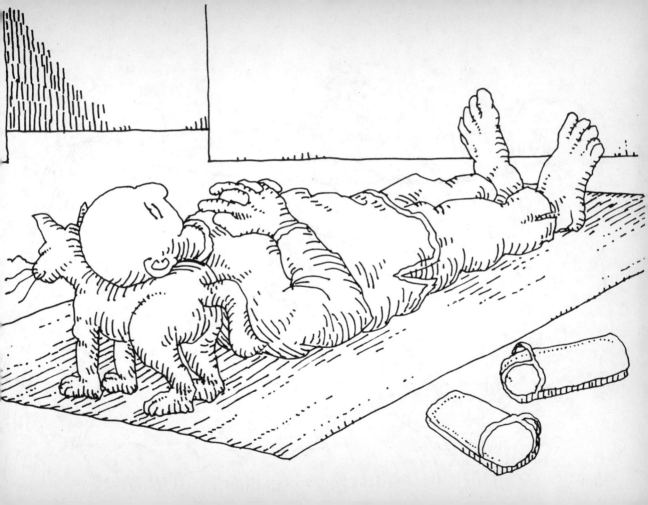

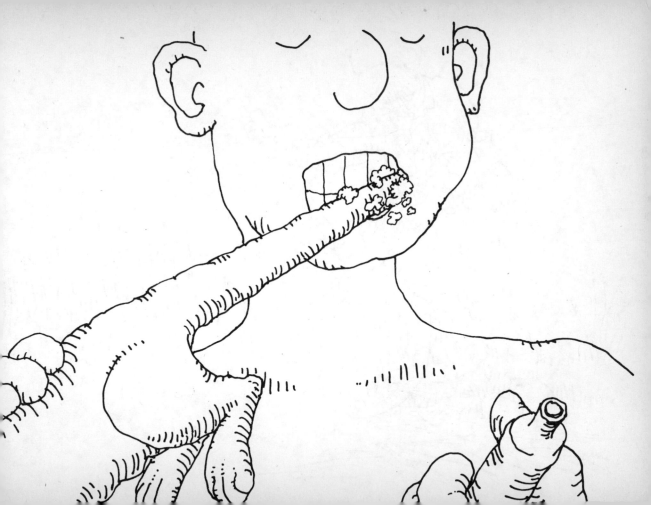

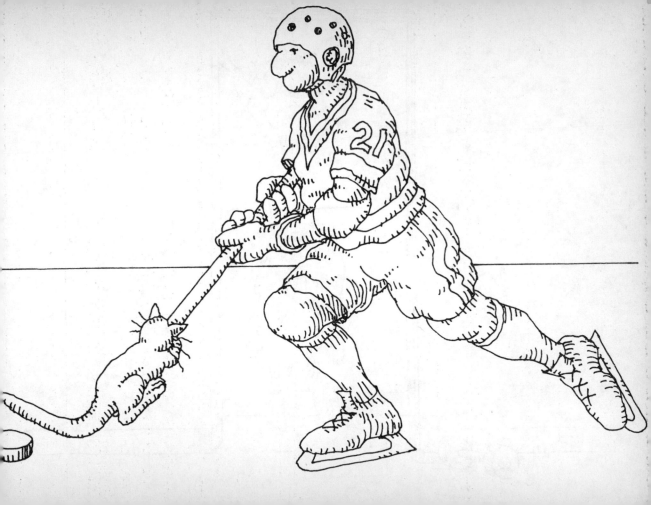

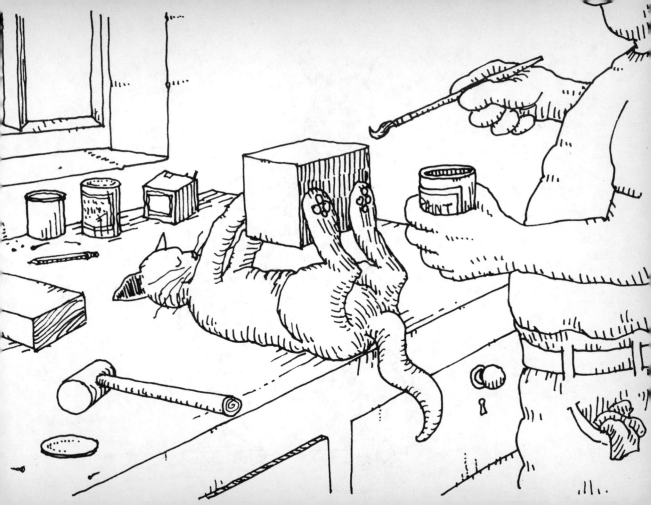

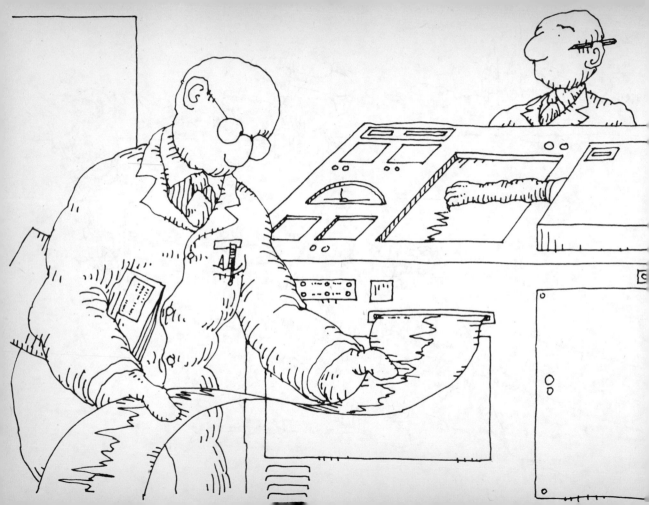

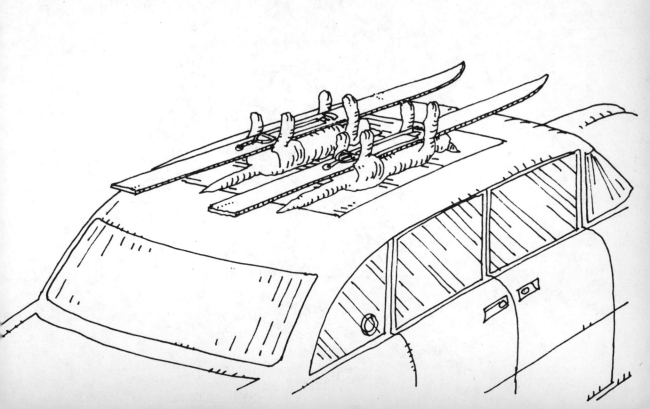

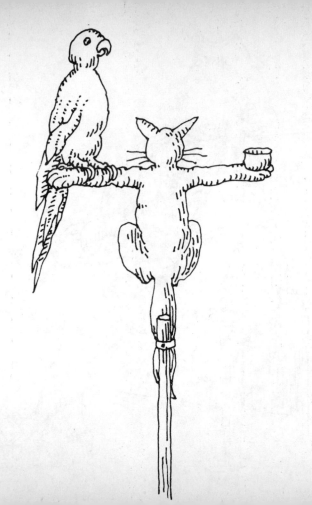

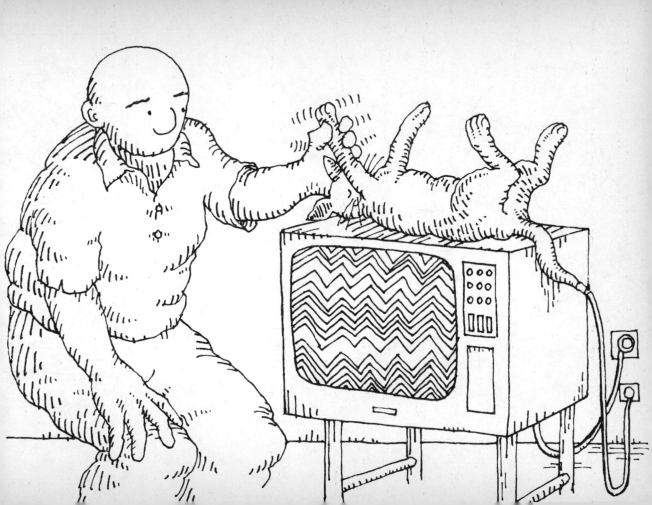

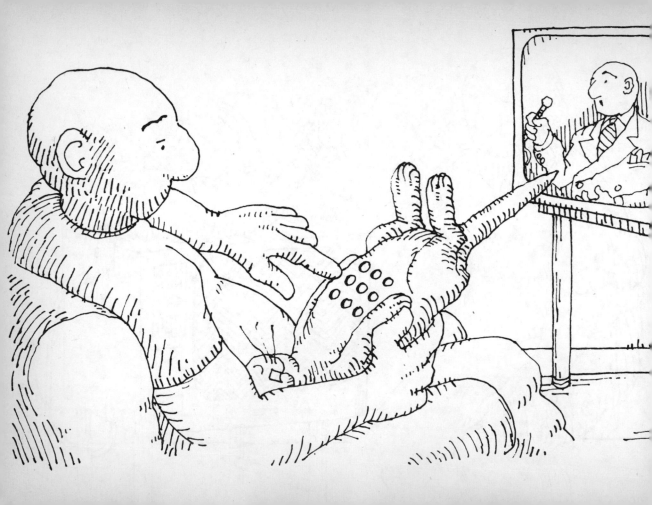

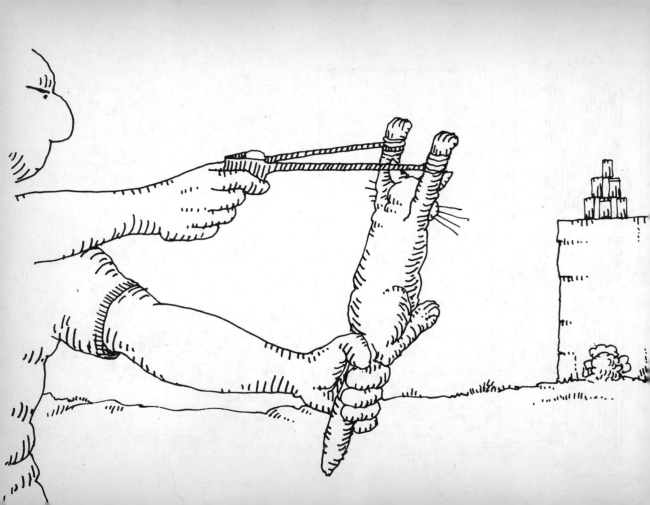

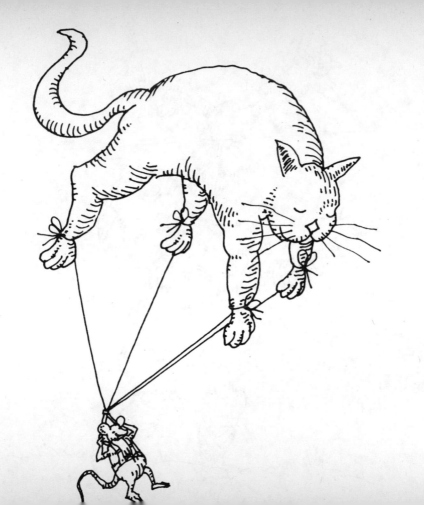

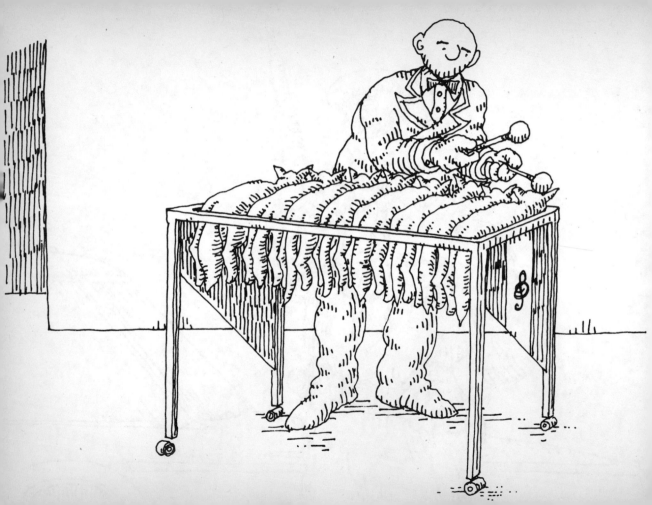

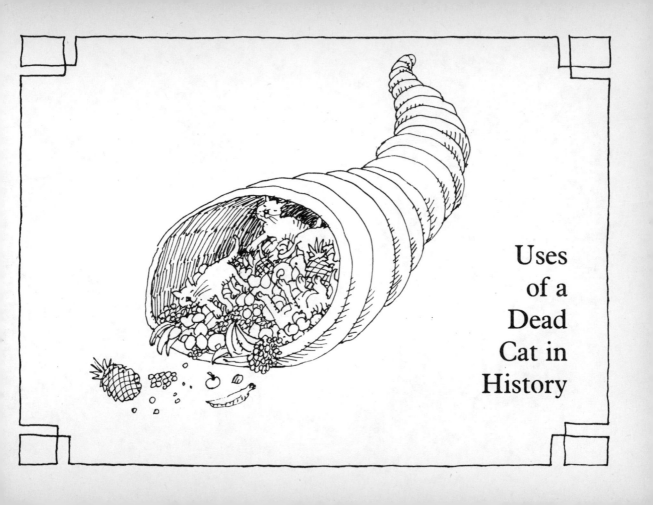

Uses
of a
Dead
Cat in
History

THE ORIGINAL CAST

NERG AND OOMA INVENT THE WHEEL

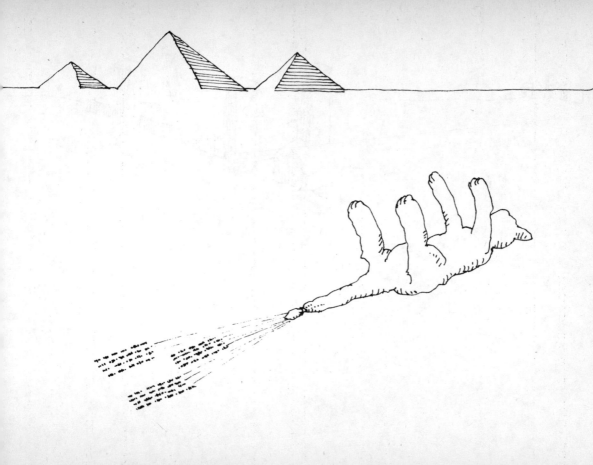

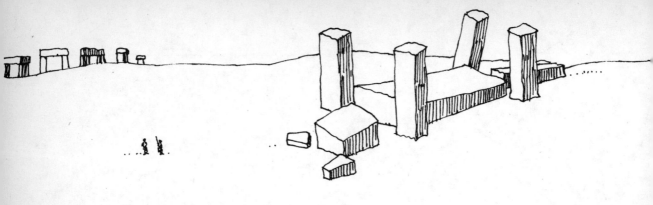

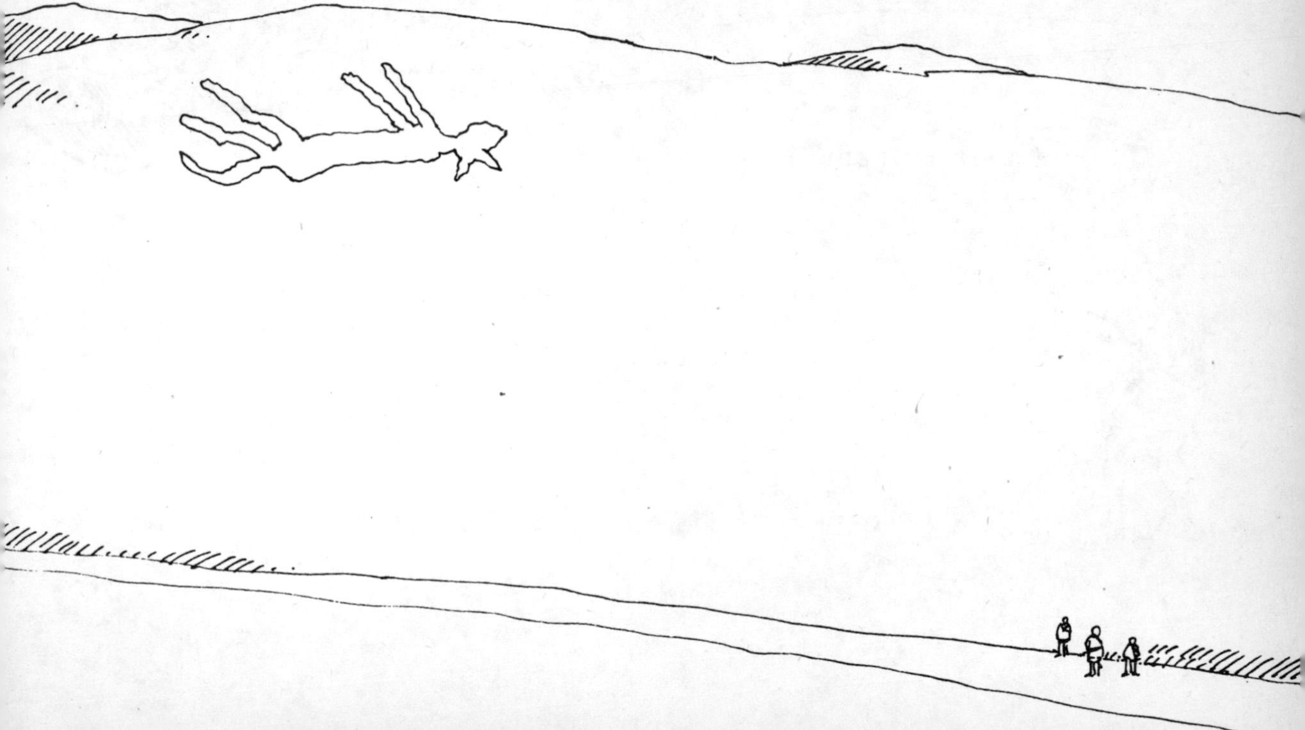

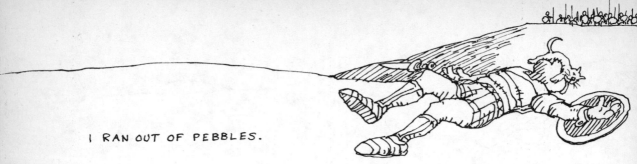

I RAN OUT OF PEBBLES.

AND AFTER THE PLAGUE OF LOCUSTS...

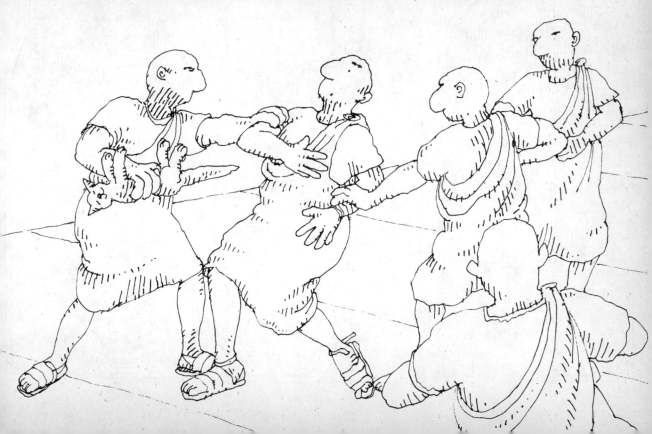

JESUS HAS A PRACTICE
BEFORE RAISING LAZARUS

'I think you'd better do the fish again.'

1493

CHRISTOPHER COLUMBUS DISCOVERS
A USE FOR THE POTATO

1588

'They don't roll very well, Sir Francis.'

PSSSST!

'Er . . . do you have anything else?'

1667

ISAAC NEWTON IS REMINDED ABOUT GRAVITY

GULLIVER MAKES ANOTHER DISCOVERY

...BECAUSE IT'S QUIET
AND DOESN'T EAT MUCH.

1752

'It's got a message, Master . . . but I don't think we should touch it.'

MONSTROSITIES of 1821

OLIVER DOES NOT ASK FOR MORE

...AND PROBABLY WITH A
REASONABLY BLUNT INSTRUMENT.

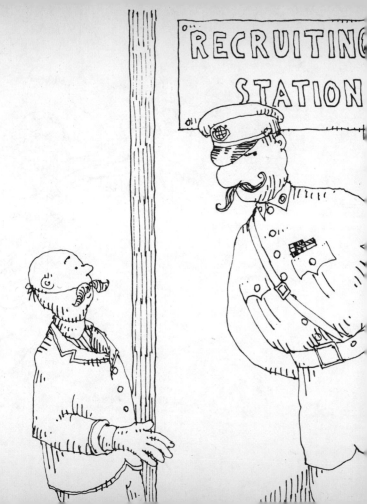

MOSCOW 1917

LUNCH IS SERVED AT THE KENNEL CLUB

MUNICH 1923

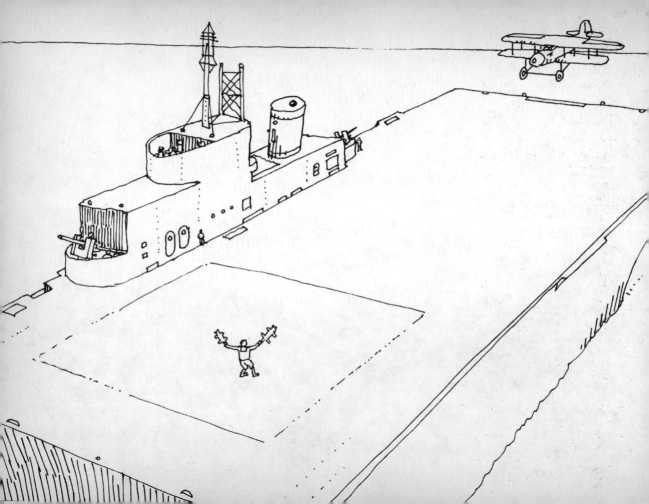

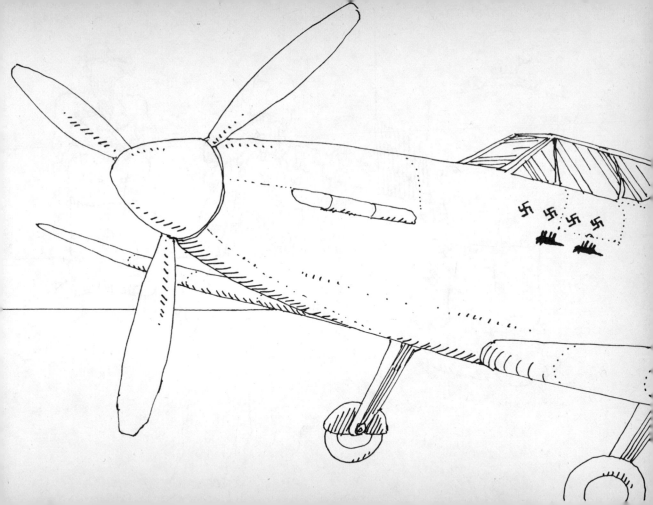

DIMBO

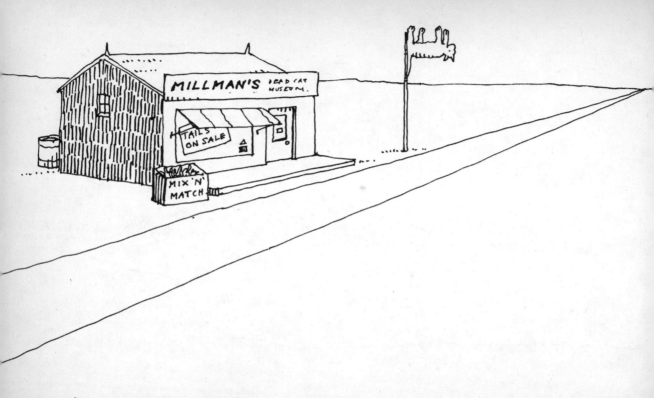

MILLMAN'S DEAD CAT MUSEUM & CURIO SHOPPE (WOOLALOONA FLATS. N.S.W. AUSTRALIA)

FELIX MORT LODGE
TITUSVILLE, NEBRASKA, 1952

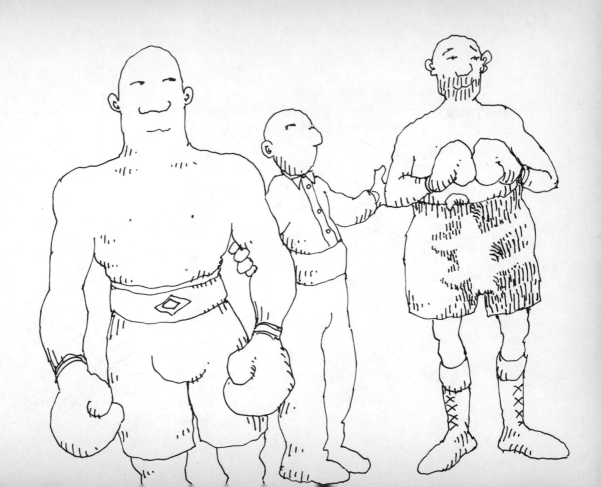

1957

SPUTNIK

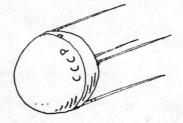

CATNIK

SHE LOVES YOU

YEAH YEAH YEAH ....

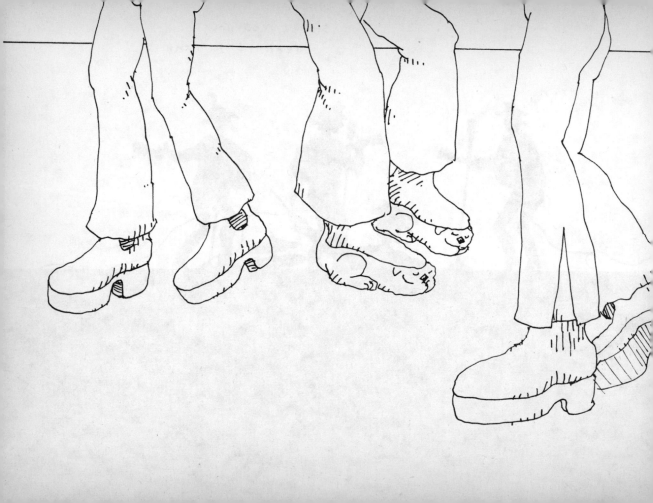

1979

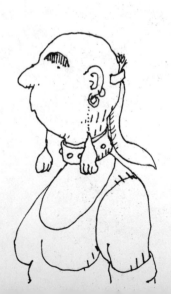

HARLEM
GLOBETROTTERS [648]
DEAD CATS [2]

MANILA
1985

1987

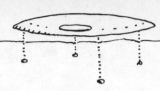